DATE DUE			

Pebble Plus

Exploring the Galaxy
Mercury

by Thomas K. Adamson

Consulting Editor: Gail Saunders-Smith, Ph.D.

Consultant: James Gerard
Aerospace Education Specialist, NASA
Kennedy Space Center, Florida

Capstone press
Mankato, Minnesota

Pebble Plus is published by Capstone Press
151 Good Counsel Drive, P.O. Box 669, Mankato, Minnesota 56002
http://www.capstone-press.com

1 2 3 4 5 6 08 07 06 05 04 03

Library of Congress Cataloging-in-Publication Data
Adamson, Thomas K., 1970–
    Mercury / by Thomas K. Adamson.
    p. cm.—(Pebble Plus: exploring the galaxy)
    Summary: Simple text and photographs describe the planet Mercury.
    Includes bibliographical references and index.
    ISBN 0-7368-2114-7 (hardcover)
    1. Mercury (Planet)—Juvenile literature. [1. Mercury (Planet)] I. Title. II. Series.
QB611 .A33 2004
523.41—dc21   2002155609

Editorial Credits
Mari C. Schuh, editor; Kia Adams, designer; Alta Schaffer, photo researcher; Eric Kudalis, product planning editor

Photo Credits
Digital Vision, 5 (Venus)
NASA, 4 (Pluto), 13, 15; JPL, 5 (Jupiter); JPL/Caltech, 5 (Uranus), 11, 17
PhotoDisc Inc., cover, 4 (Neptune), 5 (Mars, Mercury, Earth, Sun, Saturn); 9 (both), 19; Stock Trek, 1; PhotoDisc Imaging, 7
Photo Researchers/Frank Zullo, 21

Note to Parents and Teachers

The Exploring the Galaxy series supports national science standards related to earth science. This book describes and illustrates the planet Mercury. The photographs support early readers in understanding the text. The repetition of words and phrases helps early readers learn new words. This book also introduces early readers to subject-specific vocabulary words, which are defined in the Glossary section. Early readers may need assistance to read some words and to use the Table of Contents, Glossary, Read More, Internet Sites, and Index/Word List sections of the book.

Word Count: 126
Early-Intervention Level: 15

Table of Contents

Mercury 4

Mercury's Size 8

Mercury's Surface 10

People and Mercury 18

Glossary 22

Read More 23

Internet Sites 23

Index/Word List 24

Mercury

Mercury is the closest planet to the Sun. Mercury moves around the Sun faster than any other planet.

The Solar System

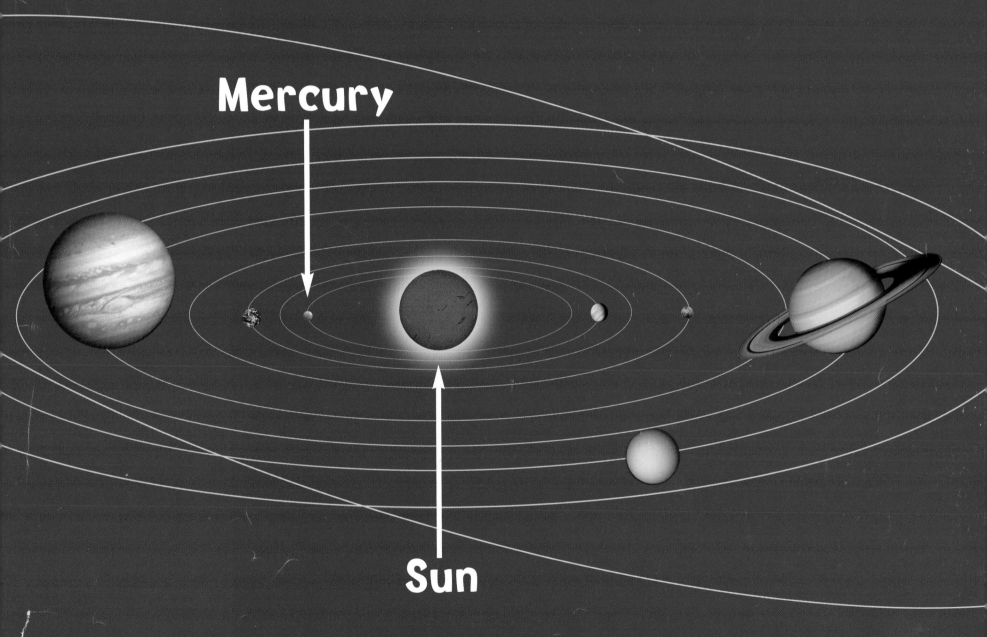

Mercury

Sun

Mercury can be colder than a freezer at night. Mercury can be hotter than an oven during the day.

Mercury's Size

Mercury is the second smallest planet. Earth is three times wider than Mercury.

Earth

Mercury

Mercury's Surface

Mercury is a rocky planet.

The surface of Mercury

looks like Earth's moon.

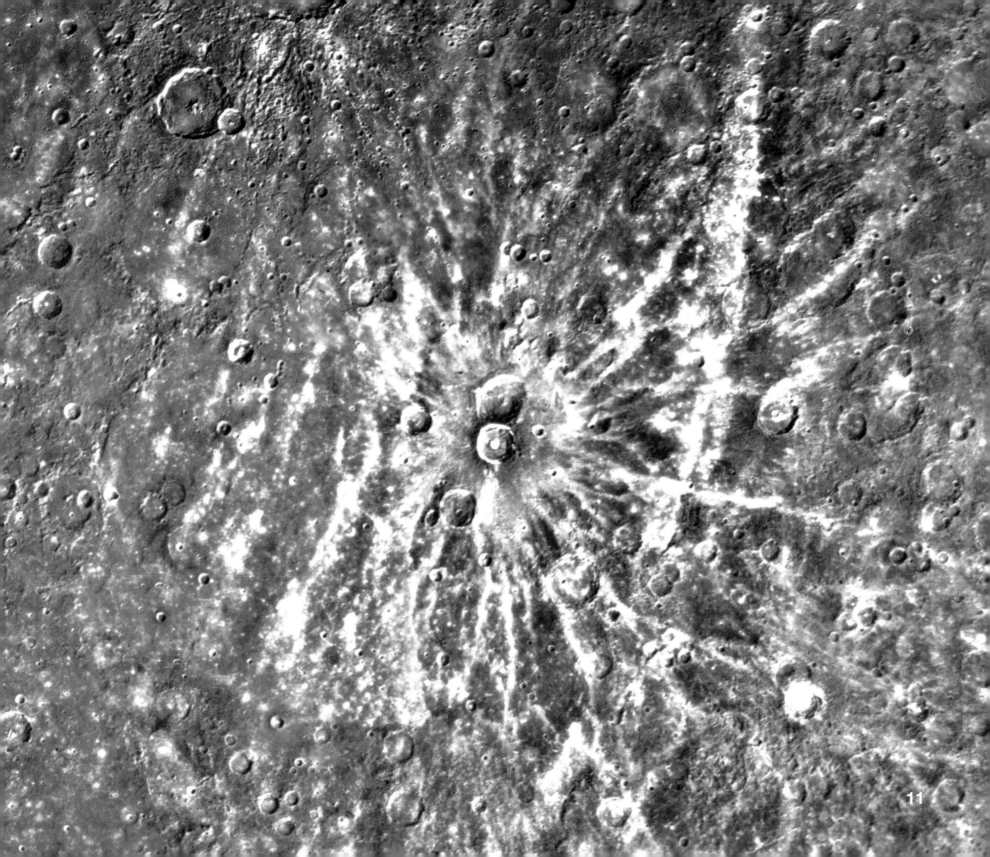

11

Mercury's surface looks gray.

Dust covers the surface.

13

Craters cover Mercury's
surface. Large rocks called
asteroids made these holes.

15

Craters near the planet's poles have ice. Sunlight cannot shine on the ice to melt it.

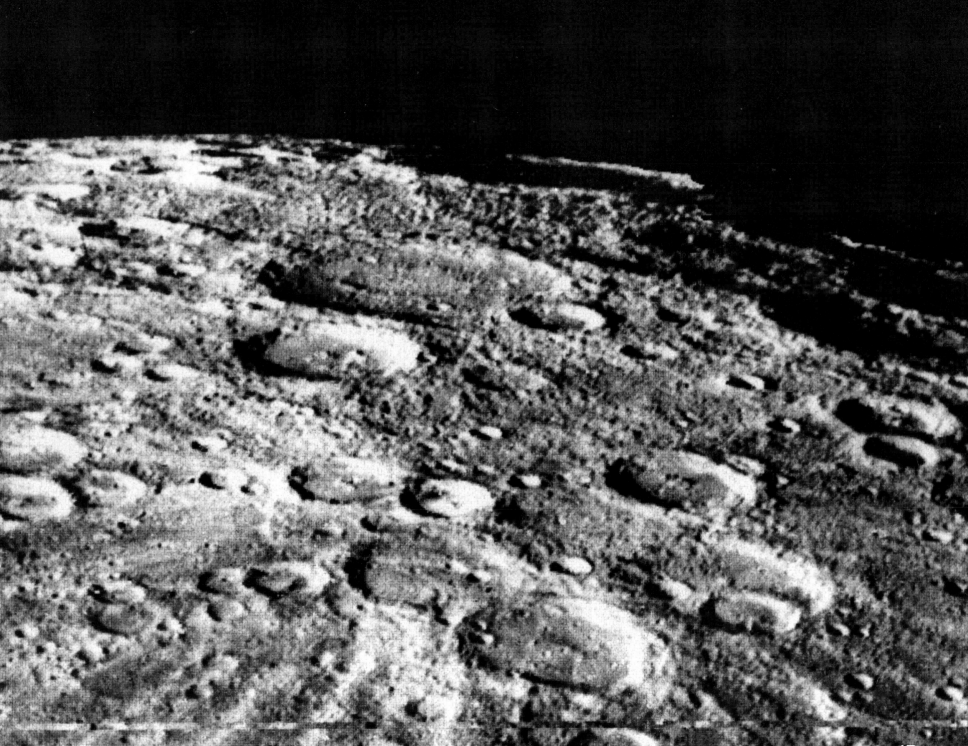

17

People and Mercury

Mercury does not have
air or water. People
and animals could not
live on Mercury.

People can sometimes
see Mercury from Earth.
Mercury looks like a dim star.

Mercury ⟶

Glossary

asteroid—a large space rock that moves around the Sun

crater—a large bowl-shaped hole in the ground

dim—somewhat dark; dim stars are not very bright.

moon—an object that moves around a planet; Earth has one moon; Mercury does not have any moons.

planet—a large object that moves around the Sun; Mercury is the closest planet to the Sun.

pole—the top or bottom part of a planet

star—a large ball of burning gases in space; the Sun is a star.

Sun—the star that the planets move around; the Sun provides light and heat for the planets.

Read More

Goss, Tim. *Mercury*. The Universe. Chicago: Heinemann Library, 2003.

Margaret, Amy. *Mercury*. The Library of the Planets. New York: PowerKids Press, 2001.

Rau, Dana Meachen. *Mercury*. Our Solar System. Minneapolis: Compass Point Books, 2002.

Internet Sites

Do you want to find out more about Mercury and the solar system? Let FactHound, our fact-finding hound dog, do the research for you.

Here's how:

1) Visit *http://www.facthound.com*

2) Type in the **Book ID** number: **0736821147**

3) Click on **FETCH IT**.

FactHound will fetch Internet sites picked by our editors just for you!

Index/Word List

air, 18

animals, 18

asteroids, 14

cover, 12, 14

craters, 14, 16

dim, 20

dust, 12

Earth, 8, 10, 20

freezer, 6

gray, 12

holes, 14

ice, 16

live, 18

moon, 10

night, 6

oven, 6

people, 18, 20

planet, 4, 8, 10, 16

rocks, 14

star, 20

Sun, 4

sunlight, 16

surface, 10, 12, 14

water, 18